Surrender

September 2, 1945

James L. Starnes
with Suzanne Simon Dietz

Layout, cover, and design by BeauDesigns.

First Edition 2014.

ISBN: 978-0-9841395-4-5

Part of Starnes' story is being reprinted from *My True Course* Dutch Van Kirk, Northumberland to Hiroshima.

PO Box 496 • Youngstown, NY 14174
www.BeauDesigns.biz

To all those lost at sea in the service of their country

CONTENTS

OTHER BOOKS BY
SUZANNE SIMON DIETZ

FOREWORD

Surrender is a poignant reflection of the joy one feels when the fight is over, when, in Jim Starnes words to me, "For the first time in decades the world was at peace," and in General MacArthur's memorable, "The entire world lies quietly at peace." Yes. It was a time of "sweet surrender." It was a time when destruction ceases, when fear no longer pervades one's being and when mankind might perceive a harmonious future with itself. But alas, it was not to be, for soon the drums of war burst forth again, and we found ourselves in Korea, Vietnam, Iraq, Bosnia, Afghanistan, and Iraq again, and then Afghanistan still.

When will we ever learn the harsh truth that War is the most harmful and destructive way to resolve conflict and that there can be a better and less costly way? Perhaps one day we can learn to live with one another. But at this point in world history, that does not seem likely.

As Jesus told us some two thousand years ago: "And ye shall hear of wars and rumors of war: see that ye be not troubled: for all of these things must come to pass, but the end is not yet." *King James Bible* Matthew 24:6.

— William O. Miller,
Rear Admiral, JAGC, US Navy (Ret)

INTRODUCTION

German armored divisions with more than a million troops tore into neighboring Poland on September 1, 1939, the second of September Japanese Standard Time (JST), beginning a conflict that drew almost every country on Earth into its midst.

Within two days Great Britain, France, India, Australia, and New Zealand declared war on Germany followed shortly by the Union of South Africa and Canada. Poland had already declared war. Once Japan attacked Pearl Harbor on December 7, 1941, most other nations joined the fight.

After six years on September 2, 1945, and more than seventy-two million deaths, possibly one hundred million according to some historians, the USS *Missouri* hosted the signatories to the formal end of the Second World War.

This souvenir booklet about the surrender ceremony of the Empire of Japan to the Allies is told through my personal story as navigator and Officer of the Deck on the battleship *Missouri* on the second of September.

The momentous event was unprecedented history bringing an end to World War II and the global fight for freedom and General MacArthur's words for peace to be "restored to the world and that God will preserve it always."

It is my hope that the reader will find this booklet helpful and bring an appreciation to the significance of September 2, 1945.

— James L. Starnes,
Lt. Commander USNR (Ret)

1

USS *BOISE*

One evening in the summer of 1940 at the age of nineteen, I made the irrevocable decision to become a naval officer. This life changing decision resulted from a short conversation with a friend. Henry Harris told me about a new officer-training program for men with at least two years of college. Henry was so excited about his decision to join the Navy and see the world. The more he talked, the more exciting it sounded. The possibility of war existed, but that though seemed so far away and of little importance. I had just completed my second year at Emory University.

Convincing my parents later that night that I should have their permission to do this was not as difficult as I first thought.[1] It did not start out well. I walked into our house about midnight. My father said, "I have heard about Henry Harris and if you are thinking of going into the Navy with him, the answer is NO!"

This became one of my first learning experiences in being persuasive. I told my parents about all the positive things I had heard about being an officer and a gentlemen to offset the negative impressions from occasional stories of drunken sailors. I knew that I would become the officer and a gentleman. When my parents heard this and knew how determined I was to pursue this course, they gave me their unconditional approval.

After passing the physical, I was inducted into the Naval Reserve in July and then served aboard the USS *Illinois* for four months of training in New York which included a thirty-day cruise. At the end of the four months, the majority of students became commissioned officers. In mid-November I received my commission as an Ensign USNR.

I joined the USS *Boise* in Long Beach, California, and spent several months operating from that port.[2] This was my first time away from home for any period of time, and I was experiencing on my own the rights of passage into adulthood. In Hollywood, I saw people from all walks of life, all parts of the country, and my first Rose Bowl game.[3] My parents drove out to visit, and we shared the beauties of the California coastline. It was a wonderful life.

In the spring of '41 the *Boise* joined the Pacific Fleet at Pearl Harbor and for the next seven months we enjoyed the routine of two weeks at sea, and two weeks of fun in port. Except for one day in four when we had duty, we were off every day about noon for what we called recreation and adventure. Several of us went in together and for three hundred dollars purchased a 1930 Cadillac convertible sedan. Now, we were really living.

While at Pearl we trained on how to conduct warfare and attack Japanese ships. The two weeks at sea were spent in defensive exercises to repel a Japanese attack. Always at sea and on duty days in port we practiced, practiced, practiced, except on Sunday. We were unaware that what we feared would happen, would happen on one of those Sundays when we were not prepared.

We left Pearl Harbor in mid November with a convoy of merchant ships on their way to China, which at the time was at war with Japan.[4] We were the only combat ship and our task was to protect the convoy. We operated in battle condition as if we were at war.

On the way to the Philippines, we sighted a strange ship in the distance, on the horizon, in evening at dusk. We could tell it was Japanese by its silhouette. They failed to identify 'friend or foe.' We were ready to be engaged. All night long we stayed at battle stations and the enemy stayed with us, monitoring our activities from a distance. By daybreak the ship was gone. We thought nothing more about it except, that it had been very, very strange. The date was December 3, 1941. We arrived in Manila with our convoy on the 5th of December.

Admiral (Thomas Charles) Hart, Commander of the Asiatic Fleet, knew war with Japan was imminent and believed Manila would be the target of an unprovoked attack. We were ordered to leave the next day without the merchant ships and to proceed south to the island of Cebu to wait out the expected events of the following week.

2

STATE OF WAR

December 8th, 1941, at 0500 a message was intercepted by the *Boise*. Ensign Starnes, the assistant navigator, headed to the bridge to take the four to eight watch.[5]

The captain showed me the communication from Secretary of the Navy Knox[6] and said, "Jim, old boy, we are at war with Japan." Our orders were to carry out the battle plan Able, Baker, Charlie. That is all, and nothing about what happened to cause such an event. A state of war now existed between the United States and the Imperial Empire of Japan. We did not know about Pearl Harbor.

On Christmas Eve we arrived at a small port in the Dutch East Indies and met some Naval Air Force pilots who had been at Pearl and told us what happened. We learned later that the Japanese ship we sighted earlier had been part of the screen guarding against detection of the task force on its way to Pearl.

In February (1942) the *Boise* ran aground on an uncharted shoal near the Island of Bali in the Dutch East Indies. The closest Navy yard where we could be repaired was in Bombay, India. So, for the next seven weeks we had some wonderful days of adventure enjoying life as Rudyard Kipling said when he wrote of "somewhere east of Suez." While the British Navy was experiencing some of its worst defeats and the Japanese had overrun Singapore, we hardly knew a war was going on.

In March after having been only patched up, we began the long voyage back to San Francisco to the Mare Island Navy

Yard for permanent repairs.

We were sent to Guadalcanal to join the fleet preparing for an invasion. At least that was what we thought. Arriving at Pearl Harbor, we were sent as a decoy to distract the Japanese fleet from our ships preparing to invade Guadalcanal. Our mission was to sail a great circle course from Pearl Harbor stopping at Midway Island before heading west to within five hundred miles of Tokyo as if we were leading a task force for another carrier based attack on Tokyo. Our odds of never returning from that mission must have been high. As it turned out, we arrived at our destination and turned on our floodlights. We launched two of the seaplanes with a catapult. Our mission was to imitate the Doolittle raid and let it be known that we were there. We broke radio silence trying to find the two planes.

The ploy worked. The Japanese fleet was diverted from the South Pacific and steamed full speed back toward Japan to intercept what they thought was a large attack force of US carriers. This enabled the invasion of Guadalcanal to take place without heavy naval interference from the Japanese. As for us, we lost our two planes and pilots after trying for hours to rescue them in heavily infested Japanese waters.

Failing to rescue our planes, we turned one hundred eighty degrees and at full speed got out of there. On the way back to Pearl, we were diverted and dispatched to Guadalcanal.

August 7, 1942, the Marines attacked the Solomon's and stormed the shores of the Tulagi, Guadalcanal, and the Malaita Islands.

We arrived at Milne Bay south of Guadalcanal. Aware of

our defeat at Savo Island, it began to look as if we would be unable to stop the Japanese from retaking Guadalcanal. Night after night we were told of the Tokyo Express and how they came down the slot to make it impossible for our forces to land reinforcements. Word began to spread that our task force was to be the one to stop the Tokyo Express. We received word from recon that the Jap fleet was on the way to Guadalcanal.[7]

We heard rumors and stories over what we felt was great concern within the administration over where to put the most effort in Europe or the Pacific. Fleet Admiral Ernest King wanted to keep the sea-lanes open between Pearl Harbor and Australia and stop the Japanese Navy's destroyers supplying replacement troops and supplies for their garrison on Guadalcanal by making round trips via the New Georgia Sound through the Solomon Islands.

October 11, 1942, between Savo Island and Cape Esperance off the northern point of Guadalcanal, the *Boise,* other cruisers and destroyers closed in on the Solomon Islands.

In the late evening Sunday the eleventh and the early morning hours of Monday the twelfth, I remember the excitement, not fear or panic, but a feeling of confidence that the game plan would work. My battle station was in the enclosed charthouse just behind the bridge. It was pitch black outside and there were no lights visible from the ships. I was aware of the action only by sound and not by sight. I heard our skipper Mike Moran quickly ask permission to open fire after we heard reports that unidentified ships were less than six thousand yards from us. I heard the captain give the order to open fire even before he received the reply.

We were not the flagship. Admiral (Norman) Scott was in

command. His ship did not have radar.[8] At 2300 we picked up a ship on our radar eight or nine miles away. Captain Moran was denied permission to open fire. When the ships closed in at about 4,000 yards the captain said, 'open fire.' The Navy policy was that if in danger we could start the battle. We immediately became the target of torpedoes and naval gunfire, our first experience in belly-to-belly warfare. After about fifteen minutes of active naval engagement, we did a lot of damage. But, we were damaged by one of their torpedoes and had to withdraw. Total darkness turned into total light.

It sounded like the fourth of July followed by screams and shouts, "We hit him. We hit him." And then, we knew we had been hit. "Flood the forward magazines" was shouted over the telephone wire of the damage control crews. We felt the ship shake as the forward magazines exploded and knew we were in danger of sinking. Somehow we knew there was a job to do. We didn't think at that time about who had been killed or injured or of our own fate. The action lasted for what seemed like an eternity, but was maybe fifteen or twenty minutes.

I knew we had sunk or badly damaged several Japanese ships. Later we thought it was eight ships. We were badly damaged ourselves listing severely to starboard. The skipper told us we were withdrawing, reducing speed, and that we must save the ship. All of a sudden there was no more battle with an enemy, just the battle to survive against the sea. The leaking was stopped and we limped away. Dawn found us alone, but safe and on our way to Milne Bay. I think somehow the mind has safety valves, and we shut out the horror of the violence, death, and carnage, or it would have been unbearable. Instead, we thought of the completion of a mission and the necessity of being ready to tackle the next one.

While routine reports were prepared, the captain and my boss, the navigator, wondered how to refer to this action. Looking at the chart where I had plotted the courses of the previous evening, I said, "Here is where it took place. We will have to call it the Battle of Cape Esperance." And so it was. This ended my one and only action in a ship-to-ship naval battle during World War II. Nothing ever compared to the violence experienced that night in October.

An enemy shell had detonated in the *Boise* forward magazines from the Japanese *Aoba* and *Kinugasa*. The ship limped back through the Panama Canal to the Philadelphia Navy yard for repairs. The explosions and burning gases killed 104 men and 3 officers and wounded about 200 sailors.[9] The *Boise*'s prominent role in the Battle of Cape Esperance helped turn back a Japanese cruiser-destroyer force en route to bombard the Marines on Guadalcanal.[10] This turning point in the war was also known as the Battle of Iron Bottom Bay because of the uncounted ships lost in the waters of the Bay.

July 9, 1943, Operation Husky, the code name for the Allied Invasion of Sicily began a large scaled amphibious and airborne operation. More than 2,500 vessels transporting troops and escorts gathered near the Oran Harbor.[11]

The USS *Boise* painted with camouflaged colors had headed for the European Theatre in late spring. She sailed through Gibraltar to Oran and Algiers to transport troops and join the fleet to invade Sicily for the first major invasion in Europe. We had unfortunate incidents shooting our own planes; there was a lot of friendly fire. The invasion of Sicily went quickly. At Salerno the German buzz bombs created a great screeching sound and a lot of fear.[12] The USS *Brooklyn*, *Philadelphia*, and *Savannah* also provided gunfire support to the landing troops.

September 3, 1943, the Allies landed in Italy.

Sometime in April, 1944, the *Boise* was in the waters around Ulithi Atoll north of Australia when I received an order to return to San Francisco Naval Base for further orders. Detached from our ship a group of us became passengers aboard a Dutch freighter for a leisurely cruise to San Francisco. We played a lot of bridge. Every night we heard, "This is Captain Rommel . . ." Usually several officers joined him for a cold beer. We asked him if he had any relationship to a very famous German general, Field Marshal Erwin Rommel. The captain said, "He is my brother" and explained that a lot of Dutch were not Nazis and that he was fighting a war against Japan in the Pacific.

Starnes reported to the Naval Base and was given a thirty-day leave.

I called in everyday and eventually was told to report to Newport, Rhode Island. I was home on leave on D-Day June 6, 1944, and left a day or two later for my second tour of duty. My second duty assignment was to head the naval navigation school to teach the new crews being quickly put out to sea.

Married now and with a child, Starnes thought the war was over for him. "I was running a naval training school in Newport, Rhode Island, for all the navigation crews of the new ships. Every week a new class started. The crews were needed because ships were being built so fast. I didn't flunk anyone. I trained the navigation crews for the *Missouri* and as head of the navigation school received the appointment as navigator of the battleship."

April 4, 1944, The Twentieth Army Air Force deployed to the Pacific Theater and operated initially from bases in India and staging bases in China, and later from the Marianas Islands.

3

USS *MISSOURI*

Early November, 1944, I received a telephone call. "Jim, old boy, you got your orders." What ship, I asked. The response was the *Missouri*. Orders were usually to "proceed and report," but this was "report right now." The *Missouri* was in New York. I got my parents to pick up my family. It was just before the presidential election in 1944.

The *Battleship Missouri* by Paul Stillwell explained the Navy's creation of a new shipboard organization, which used the battleship as a test with navigation as one of the divisions.

As the navigator I kept track of where the ship went and when it got there. I was just a lieutenant. A month later I received a spot promotion to Lieutenant Commander during my eighth trip through the Panama Canal. The beam on the battleship was one hundred eight feet. The canal pilots navigated us through the one hundred ten foot locks in the canal with only one foot on each side to squeeze through. The *Missouri* entered the Pacific with the battleships *Arkansas* and the *Texas*.

November 7, 1944, Roosevelt won re-election for a fourth term as president. Construction began in Alamogordo, New Mexico, for the Trinity test site.[13]

December 24, 1944, the USS *Missouri* arrived at Pearl Harbor on Christmas Eve and its welcome to the Pacific Fleet.

February 19, 1945, aboard the *Missouri* at Iwo Jima, it was a whole day of bombardment before the Landing Craft headed for the shores, but the Japs were caved in. It was one of the most horrible battles.

The order for *Operation Detachment* was given to "Land the Landing Force" sending waves of Marines to the southern beaches of the island of Iwo Jima also known as Sulphur Island. The previous three days of naval and aerial barrage on Iwo filled the air with smoke as strong swells of the Pacific waters crashed on the shores.

March 24, 1945, the *Missouri* and other ships bombarded the southeast coast of Okinawa in preparation for the land invasion.

When the time came for us to act like the battleship we were, it was great, really a good feeling. While the ship was at battle stations, we ate K-rations of canned meat or cheese.

April 5, 1945, Moscow denounced Japan for waging war against its allies the United States and Great Britain and that it would not renew the Soviet-Japan neutrality pact. Coinciding with Moscow's announcement, Premier Gen. Kuniaki Koiso and his cabinet resigned according to Tokyo Radio. Koiso, an ardent member of Japan's militarist party, had recently broadcast that Japan was prepared to fight to recapture Iwo Jima, Saipan, and Guadalcanal according to an AP report. Baron Kantaro Suzuki, a retired admiral, was appointed in place of Koiso.[14]

April 8, 1945, the Japs made the decision to go all out on the fleet with kamikazes and attacked the carriers. I was on the bridge when we were attacked. A kamikaze hit the deck level of the stern half in the water and half on the bridge. We tried to protect ourselves and lost no lives. We gave the pilot a regular Navy funeral with the part of his body that was on one half of the aircraft.

I had a cabin just aft of the bridge on the port side so I could immediately be on call.

April 12, 1945, Franklin Roosevelt, the 32nd President of the United States, died. When the news reached the ship the signalman lowered the flag to half-mast.

April 16, 1945, the *Missouri* endured twelve hours of air attacks.

May 18, 1945, Admiral William Halsey, Jr., broke his flag aboard the *Missouri.*

July 8, 1945, the Third Fleet set course to approach the Japanese main islands targeting Tokyo on July 10th and several days later on Honshu and Hokkaido.[15] The *Missouri* fired several hundred rounds at the steel works.

For several days in mid July, the attacks continued targeting the industrial areas on the Island of Honshu. Starnes relied on the new Loran electronic navigation system during the night bombardment. Captain (Stuart "Sunshine") Murray was confident in his navigator and took Starnes' recommendation to change course off the enemy's coast. Lt. Commander James L. Starnes was responsible for navigating the Third Fleet.

Captain Murray asked me, "Are we there yet Jimmy?" Finally we headed towards the shore through obstacles. The captain was anxious and asked the question again. I had been trained to have so much confidence and felt that I could beat the world. We turned parallel to the shore with no resistance.

Plans were being made for the invasion of Japan on

Kyushu when we received the news that the B-29 *Enola Gay* had dropped an atomic bomb on Hiroshima.

On August 9, 1945, aboard the *Missouri* Admiral Halsey said, "Looks like it is coming to an end." A day or two later we got word that the *Missouri* was going to be the place where the surrender would take place. I thought we should get out our swords and shine them.

A few days before, we took the ship into Sagami Bay and could see Mount Fuji. Japanese river pilots led us into Tokyo Bay to avoid mine fields. We called the pilot Mr. Moto. He spoke impeccable English. All of a sudden we went from hatred and death to friendship. We asked him questions. Could we go into Tokyo? Were some Japanese sore losers? He responded, "The Emperor said . . ." We anchored in the bay, not moored. The destroyers brought the press on the port side.

4

SEPTEMBER 2, 1945

September 2, 1945, I was the Officer of the Deck from 0800 to 1200. Every four hours there was a different Officer of the Deck, third in command under the captain and the executive officer. My job was to make sure we did not screw up.[16]

Photo SC 211865 from the Army Signal Corps Collection in the National Archives.
Left to right, Lt. Doug Plate, Captain Murray, Lt. Commander James L. Starnes, and Rear Admiral Richard E. Byrd, USN, boarding the USS *Missouri* for the surrender ceremonies in Tokyo Bay, Japan, 2 September 1945.

We flew the flag of the top most Commander aboard: first, Halsey, a four star admiral, then Nimitz's, a five star admiral; we hauled down Halsey's flag, and raised MacArthur's, a five star general, twin flags.

The Deck Log-Remarks Sheet signed by J. L. Starnes, Lt. Comdr., U.S.N.R., reported on 08-12:

"Anchored as before. 0803, USS *Buchanan* (DD484) came alongside to port with various general officers of the Army and foreign representatives to witness surrender ceremonies. 0805, Fleet Admiral C. W. Nimitz came aboard and his personal flag was broken at the mainmast. 0824, USS *Buchanan* (DD484) cast off. 0838, USS *Nicholas* (DD449) came alongside to port with General of the Army Douglas MacArthur.[17] 0843, General of the Army Douglas MacArthur came aboard and his personal flag was broken at the mainmast alongside the personal flag of Fleet Admiral C. W. Nimitz. 0848, USS *Nicholas* (DD449) cast off."[18]

The admiral's barge brought the Japanese officials.[19] Eight side boys, four on each side stood at the top of the gangplank. I chose the eight men, each more than six feet tall. (Another detail to intimidate the Japanese delegation.)

The Japanese asked permission to come aboard, and we responded, "permission granted." Halsey and Nimitz took the Japanese one deck higher to the surrender deck.[20]

National Archives photo

In Tokyo Bay latitude 35° 21' 17" north, longitude 139° 45' 36" east, Gen. Douglas MacArthur and his staff watched as Mamoru Shigemitsu "by Command and behalf of the Emperor of Japan, and the Japanese government," and Gen. Yoshijiro Umezu, Chief of the Army General Staff, "by Command and in behalf of the Japanese Imperial General Headquarters," signed the terms of surrender. Gen. Douglas MacArthur, Allied Supreme Commander for the Allied Forces, signed and accepted at 0908 hours for "all nations," Fleet Adm. Chester W. Nimitz for the United States, Gen. Hsu Yung-Chang for the Republic of China, Adm. Sir Bruce Fraser for the United Kingdom, Lt. Gen. Kuzma Nikolayevich Derevyanko for the USSR, Gen. Sir Thomas Blamey for Australia, Col. Lawrence

Moore Cosgrove for Canada, Gen. Philippe Leclerc for the Provisional Government of the French Republic, Adm. C.E.L. Helfrich for the Kingdom of the Netherlands, and Air Vice Marshal Leonard M. Isitt for New Zealand.[21]

It's over. After all the devastation and cruelty, I looked up from the quarterdeck to the upper deck and could see all these Allied officers. It was a feeling of tremendous elation.

MacArthur concluded with "let us pray that peace be now restored to the world and that God will preserve it always. These proceedings are closed." According to the log the ceremony was completed at 0925.

There was a plan to have huge groups fly over the deck. MacArthur turned to Halsey and said, "Where are the damn planes?" As the Japs came off the deck the bombers blackened

National Archives photo of the USS *Missouri* on September 2, 1945

the sky. Four hundred fifty carrier planes from the Third Fleet, followed by bombers, flew overhead.[22] One of the pilots Richard C. Kahl flew "the power mission with several hundred other B-29s over the deck at about 300 feet to make a display for the Japanese. The noise was incredible."[23] The message was don't fool with us anymore.

The surrender ceremony broadcast to the world took twenty-three minutes.

The war was over!

I grew up during those five years in the Navy. My memories are filled with wonderful thoughts of all the experiences, even the unpleasant ones. My most lasting memory given the assignment of Officer of the Deck during the surrender aboard the *Missouri* is of peace and not war. After many years I am left with the belief that there must be a better way for mankind to conduct international affairs.

I have read the following statement many times and believe it to be one of the most powerful to come out of the war. Gen. Douglas MacArthur spoke to the joint meeting of Congress on April 19, 1951.

Military alliances, balances of power, leagues of nations, all in turn failed, leaving the only path to be by way of the crucible of war. The utter destructiveness of war now blocks out this alternative. We have had our last chance. If we will not devise some greater and more equitable system, our Armageddon will be at our door. The problem basically is theological and involves a spiritual recrudescence, an improvement of human character that will synchronize with our almost matchless advances in science, art, literature and all material and cultural developments of the past two thousand years. It must be of the spirit if we are to save the flesh.

5

REFLECTIONS

We had been as surprised as the rest of the world when the atomic bombs were dropped and when we heard that the *Missouri* would be the site of the formal surrender. President Truman had made the statement when she was launched that "Someday the mighty Mo would steam into Tokyo Bay with all guns blazing and the war will be over."

It was an honor to serve as Officer of the Deck at the surrender ceremony. Many have asked me how I happened to be selected. It was not a personal selection, but organizational. The navigator of a ship always became Officer of the Deck at general quarters, combat readiness, and special occasions. This was a really special occasion and plenty of professional help went into the planning.

Admiral Halsey's staff of the Third Fleet and the captain and officers of our ship were aware of the enormous amount of detail and arrangements needed to transport and accommodate the allied officers coming aboard and the representatives of the invited media and press.

We realized nothing like this had ever occurred before and knew there would be a lot to learn. One of the first thoughts was that it would be a very formal ceremony with dress whites, sabers, and all the glitter of blue and gold. However, we soon heard that MacArthur sent down the word that "we fought them in our khaki uniforms and accept their surrender in our khaki uniforms."

The *Missouri* was at anchor and not moored. Ships of

the fleet, destroyers mainly, were assembled to transport the dignitaries from their various locations including the Japanese. The ships tied up along the port side for the disembarkation of the officers and the media. The Japanese ship anchored off our starboard side so we could send the Admiral's barge and the captain's gig to bring them to the ship and climb the ladder of the gangplank including peg-legged Mamoru Shigemitsu, the Minister of Foreign Affairs. The Japanese then asked permission to come aboard from the Officer of the Deck.

My main responsibility was to delegate details to carry out the plan of the day and to write the log of the "8 to 12" watch, which included the entire ceremony. I am glad to say everything came off as planned including flying the flags of Admiral Nimitz and General MacArthur side by side from the mainmast.

After the very short but impressive ceremony, the Japanese delegation left the ship. The sky was blackened with US airplanes, as a reminder of the superior force that had brought this struggle to a successful conclusion.

At the beginning of the war, we did not know if we were going to win. Would America celebrate its last July Fourth and the battleship Yamato enter the San Francisco harbor? We darn nearly lost.

Unfathomable millions of lives had been lost in the Asian-Pacific war. American casualties from battle deaths, other deaths, and wounds exceeded a million. Casualties did not include combat related psychological disability and non-battle deaths of Navy and Marines.

If Japan had not surrendered, more lives on both sides would have been lost. The American Surgeon General had ordered almost half a million body bags for the planned land invasion. Japanese militants proclaimed the "Glorious Death of One Hundred Million" as the civilian militia prepared to fight for the Emperor.

September 2, 1945, brought a close to one of the most monumental moments in history and an end to many horrible battles, worldwide conflict, and years of Japanese aggression.

The war was over.

James L. Starnes September 2, 2005, on "Mighty Mo"

On September 2, 1945, I stood on the deck of the battleship *Missouri*. As Officer of the Deck I participated and witnessed the surrender ceremonies of the Japanese Empire to the Allied forces of the world. That time was such a special time in my life, serving in the Navy for five years, seeing combat in many places, knowing it was finally over, and that we had been victorious. Emotions were strong. Knowing that the world was now at peace was indescribable. That moment in time was a dedication to all who sacrificed their lives in hope that victory would be possible. I went back to Pearl Harbor on September 2, 2005, on the sixtieth anniversary to participate and stand again on the *Missouri* deck for the commemoration of that key moment in history, and to remember that event, which brought an end to the global conflict of World War II.

The Battleship Missouri Memorial is moored adjacent to Ford Island, an islet in Pearl Harbor, near the USS Arizona Memorial. The Arizona Memorial marks the resting place of 1,177 sailors and Marines killed on the ship during the December 7, 1941, attack on Pearl Harbor.

Battleship Missouri Memorial
63 Cowpens Street
Honolulu, Hawaii 96818
(808) 455-1600
https://www.ussmissouri.org

REMEMBER SEPTEMBER 2, 1945

That date of September 2, 1945, remains a high point in my life. I was sure then that the United States of America was an exceptional country. Almost seventy years later most Americans do not remember the significance of that date.

Remember the more than 72 million who died during World War II.

Remember the majority of about 45 million of the total deaths were civilian deaths.

Remember the 16 million men and women at arms from the United States.

Remember the sacrifice of more than one million American casualties.

Remember the 61 countries, almost all on the Earth, that participated.

Remember the 50 million refugees and displaced persons.

Remember the efforts of the US after the war to rebuild Germany and Japan, now Allies.

Remember the significance of September 2, 1945, to honor the sacrifice of the men and women who fought and died for the freedom of the world. We can contribute to society, exercise our right to vote, and do our part to preserving our way of life, our freedoms, and "one Nation under God, indivisible, with liberty and justice for all."

— James L. Starnes,
Lt. Cmdr. USNR (Ret)

ENDNOTES

[1] James L. "Jim" Starnes telephone interviews with author and Starnes memorandum to "The Budd Boys – my grandsons Chandler, Bryant, and Wesley." Starnes born in 1921 in Little Rock, Arkansas, to James L. Starnes and Maude White, grew up in Decatur, Georgia. After attending Emory University for two years he joined the Navy. Starnes graduated from a V-7 training class. "We trained as if we were at Annapolis, but it was a compacted program." Commissioned an Ensign in November 1940 Starnes chose active duty over returning to civilian life.

[2] The USS *Boise* was a Brooklyn Class light cruiser.

[3] On January 1, 1941, Stanford made football history by using the "T" formation to defeat Nebraska 21 – 14 at the Rose Bowl Game. Rose Bowl 1941, http://www.rosebowlhistory. org/rose-bowl-1941.php [accessed October 27, 2012].

[4] The *Boise* escorted troop transports. Kermit Bonner, *Final Voyage*, (Paducah, KY: Turner Publishing Co., 1996), 30.

[5] West of the International Date Line is one day ahead of HAST – Hawaii-Aleutian Standard Time Zone.

[6] Frank Knox, Secretary of the Navy, and at the age of fourteen served as a trooper with Teddy Roosevelt's Rough Riders in Cuba during the Spanish American War. Jack Alexander, "Secretary of the Navy Frank Knox," *Life* Magazine, March 10, 1941, and the Naval History and Heritage Command website.

[7] The Allied forces named the Japanese route to supply their troops the "Tokyo Express."

8 Admiral Norman Scott, buried at sea, was killed in action aboard his flagship, the cruiser *Atlanta* November 13, 1942. Winston Groom, *1942: The Year That Tried Men's Soul*, (New York: Grove Press. 2005), 302.

9 Starnes' recollections and Bonner in the *Final Voyage* described the damage to the *Boise* and the casualties during the Battle of Cape Victory at Esperance, 33, and the Naval Historical Center, http://www.history.navy.mil/photos/per-us/uspers-m/ej-moran.htm [accessed September 5, 2010].

10 Captain Edward J. "Mike" Moran assumed command of the *Boise* in late January 1942 bringing her back to the states after the ship accidentally grounded during the East Indies campaign. Moran led the ship to the South Pacific war zone for the campaign to hold Guadalcanal and awarded the Navy Cross for his "extraordinary heroism and courage" during that action. "Rear Admiral Edward J. "Mike" Moran, USN (Retired), 1893 – 1957," Dept. of the Navy – Naval Historical Center, http://www.history.navy.mil/photos/pers-us/uspers-m/ej-moran.htm [accessed September 8, 2010].

11 Kermit Bonner, *Final Voyage*, (Paducah, KY: Turner Publishing Co., 1996), 48.

12 Starnes was made navigator of the *Boise*, which headed back to the Pacific.

13 Edward T. Sullivan, *The Ultimate Weapon* The Race To Develop The Atomic Bomb, (New York, NY: Holiday House, 2007), 152.

14 Kuniakai Koiso replaced Premier Hideki Tojo in July 1944. "Crisis Makes Tokyo Form New Cabinet," *The Stars and Stripes* London Edition, April 6, 1945.

15 "We led the Fleet to Hokkaido to bomb a munitions plant," said Commander Starnes.

16 Starnes worried that the peg-legged Japanese Minister of Foreign Affairs Mamoru Shigemitsu might fall down the stairs. Bill Torpy, "65 years, just down the street," *The Atlanta*

Journal-Constitution, August 28, 2010.

[17] A letter dated September 28, 1965, from the Department of the Navy to Victor Gondos, Head, Army-Navy Branch, stated that "based on an examination of the logs and war diaries of *Buchanan* and *Nicholas* it is clear that *Buchanan* transported General MacArthur to *Missouri* for the Japanese surrender ceremonies," National Archives.

[18] Log of the *USS Missouri* for September 2, 1945, Harry S. Truman Library, Independence, MO.

[19] Foreign Minister Mamoru Shigemitsu led the Japanese emissaries.

[20] At 0856, Japanese representatives came aboard. At 0902 according to the log, the ceremony commenced and the Instrument of Surrender presented to all parties including representatives of the United States, Republic of China, United Kingdom, British Pacific Fleet, Union Soviet Socialist Republic, Commonwealth of Australia, Dominion of Canada, Republic of France, Commonwealth of New Zealand, United Kingdom of Netherlands, Japanese Empire, United States Navy, and United States Army.

[21] Deck Log of J. L. Starnes, Lt. Comdr., U.S.N.R., Harry S. Truman Library.

[22] "Surrender of Japan, 2 September 1945, Aircraft Flyover as the Ceremonies Conclude," United States Navy Naval History & Heritage Command, http://www.history.navy.mil/index.html [accessed August 30, 2010].

[23] Richard C. Kahl, interview with Dietz, Youngstown, NY, for *Honor Thy Fathers & Mothers* publication, May 17, 2007. Kahl assigned to a B-29 bomber group on Tinian participated in the incendiary bombing raids on Japanese cities. Prior to the briefings for the B-29s missions, the bartender at the Officer's Club, a Japanese POW, correctly identified for Kahl the "secret" targets.

JAMES L. STARNES

James L. Starnes was born in Little Rock, Arkansas, in 1921. His family eventually moved to Decatur, Georgia, where he attended Decatur Boys High School.

On January 15, 1943, Jim married his childhood sweetheart Rose Courtenay. After the war, Jim attended Emory's Lamar School of Law at night while working during the day to support his family. After seventeen years of marriage and four children, Rose passed away from cancer at the age of thirty-eight.

Starnes met and married Betty Hughen in 1961 and adopted her three children. Betty passed away in 2010.

Jim's neighbor and friend Henry Harris planned to attend Theology school after the war. Harris was killed at the Battle of Guadalcanal.

Lt. Commander James L. Starnes, envisioned himself as part of the poem "By Nimitz – and Halsey – and Me" written in September 1945 by Captain Gordon Beecher.

The poem concluded with "remember Pearl Harbor" and a warning to the Japanese to never start war again for "We have a country with millions of men like Nimitz — and Halsey — and me." For the Officer of the Deck on the *Missouri* on September 2, 1945, the last line is "Nimitz — and Halsey — and Starnes."

On-line YouTube Video

"Japanese Sign Final Surrender 1945 Newsreel"
http://www.youtube.com/watch?v=p09gugpF_hE

ABOUT THE AUTHOR

Suzanne Simon Dietz is the historian for the Aero Club of Buffalo and the Town of Porter in New York State. She has lectured in Western New York on local history topics and in particular German prisoners of war held at Fort Niagara in the Town of Porter during World War II.

Dietz is the authorized biographer of Dutch Van Kirk, the last living crewman of the *Enola Gay* that dropped the atomic bomb on Hiroshima, which helped bring an end to World War II. Van Kirk passed away July 28, 2014.

Mrs. Dietz researches and writes for the Niagara Aerospace Museum. The author's father, the late John Victor Simon, served during the Second World War as a scout in the United States Army with the 353rd Regiment, 89th Infantry Division.

www.SuzanneSimonDietz.com